TALES OF AN AFRICAN ENTREPRENEUR

The Best Of

I0493039

By Tiisetso Maloma

PUBLISHING AND COPYRIGHT

TALES OF AN AFRICAN ENTREPRENEUR

Copyright © 2016 Tiisetso Maloma

ISBN print: 978-1535103138

ISBN eBook: 978-1-365-23788-1

Published by Maloma Content

Book conversion, online distribution and layout by www.bulabuka.co.za

Author website www.tiisetsomaloma.com

FOLLOW ME

Social Media @tiisetsomaloma

Blog (subscribe to newsletter): **www.tiisetsomaloma.com**

CONTENTS

THE AUTHOR

I am a writer, entrepreneur, devised EBC Business Model, and author of 3 books: The Anxious Entrepreneur, Forget The business Plan Use This Short Model and Township Biz Fastrack.

- -

I became disillusioned with business plans, by their rigidity and tediousness, so I devised a short and easy model to use instead called EBC. It became the book Forget The Business, Plan Use This Short Model.

I knew that how township businesses are started and grown provide the best and fascinating blueprint of lessons on starting an entrepreneurship venture; these are techniques any good start-up in the world employs to find traction and growth. I wrote a simple dissertation – which is the book Township Biz Fastrack.

I am the most anxious person you can meet and I heal it with creativity. It is all in my 3rd book, The Anxious Entrepreneur: Anxiety Defeats Creativity - Creativity Defeats Anxiety.

So far, I have done and achieved almost all the things I wanted in a short period of time (almost 10 years): accountant, DJ, author, clothing labels, television, technology and a few other things.

I have interesting stories on my continuing entrepreneurship journey. Certainly the route has been faulty and with many brutal accidents. I tell it all on my blog here tiisetsomaloma.com. Make sure to subscribe.

Today I am involved in various businesses entities: networking (STARTUP PICNIC), publishing (Bula Buka and Maloma Publishing), developing business courses, consulting and a few others. I am what is called 'parallel entrepreneur'.

Key attributes

- Successfully founded/started and project managed several start-ups with no resources.
- Picking resources to deliberately do without and minimum viability essentials to gain traction with.
- Led a few successful marketing campaigns with zero budget.

Media appearances

Through our entrepreneurship activism, I was read, seen or heard on Under30CEO, Power FM, SAFM, NSBC, How We Made It in Africa, Business Report, Destiny Man Magazine, Cliff Central, Radio 2000 FM, YFM, SABC, Mogul in the Making, and other outlets.

Education

Diploma in Accounting and a Post Graduate Diploma in Forensic Auditing (2008), both with the University of Johannesburg.

Worked with

I proudly served various good companies in one way or another: SAICA's The Hope Factory, Ndalo Media, Nedbank, SABC, ACM Gold, The Hope Factory, CSIR, Soul City, Moshito, Meerkat Media and others.

ABOUT THE BOOK

TALES OF AN AFRICAN ENTREPRENEUR is a collection of some of Tiisetso Maloma's best rated posts spanning over 7 years. He is a parallel entrepreneur, author and writer from South Africa.

In his most-times-anecdotal and uncanny writing, the book shares entrepreneurship and self-help lessons.

Popular articles included are: DATING ADVICE THAT CAN SAVE YOUR BUSINESS FROM A NO GAME ENTREPRENEUR, HOW MY GRANDMOTHER AND HER DAUGHTER (MY MOTHER) RUINED MY FIRST BUSINESSES AND THE REASONS WHY PEOPLE DO NOT WANT YOU TO FOLLOW YOUR DREAMS.

Being an entrepreneur in Africa is a different business. Most popular and outstanding entrepreneurship stories come from The West, and their application doesn't always fit. TALES OF AN AFRICAN ENTREPRENEUR unintentionally helps fill the gap.

His entrepreneurship profile includes careers he always wanted to pursue and did: accounting, DJ'ing, publishing, clothing, television, technology and a few others.

An entrepreneurship journey has countless failures, discoveries and lessons. Tiisetso says his is heightened with these experiences due to practising parallel entrepreneurship, which is starting and at the same time operating more than one venture.

By consequence of ever starting and running more than one business, he has honed the following skills which the book shares:

- Starting a business the fastest.
- And with almost no funds and resources.
- Picking resources to do without and the minimal essentials to least do with in order to get a business on the road.

- Marketing a business successfully without budget.
- Managing entrepreneurship anxieties.

OTHER BOOKS BY AUTHOR

FORGET THE BUSINESS PLAN USE THIS SHORT MODEL  www.tiisetsomaloma.com/forgetplan	THE ANXIOUS ENTREPRENEUR  www.tiisetsomaloma.com/anxiousbook
TOWNSHIP BIZ FASTRACK  www.tiisetsomaloma.com/townshipbiz	

HOW MY GRANDMOTHER AND HER DAUGHTER, MY MOTHER, RUINED MY FIRST BUSINESSES

When it rained, with my very clean school uniform, I would walk into the pool of rainwater outside our front yard. Sometimes I would throw my grandma with stones. This was all in protest not to go to school.

Such tendencies made sure I went through Sub A to standard 1 by the whip, grade 1 to 3 as it known today. The rod wasn't spared. The child didn't perish. S/O to Kwanamoloto Primary School.

1993. I was 6 or 7 years old. I still wet my bed and I stayed with "mma", my grandma.

I saved up money to buy vegetable seeds: carrots, cabbage and spinach. With passion and hard work I nursed my little farm. We didn't have running water, most of the houses didn't. Actually none of the houses in the area did.

Every (or most) morning after noticing that I had wet my bed, it would be a reminder to water my garden. I did.

When my garden had ripe fresh produce, neighbours came to ask for my veggies. My grandma, she is sweet, she gave them a bit. They were poor. To come to think about it, we were poor as well – mud houses and stuff. I dint know we were poor.

A bit for everyone was all of my produce. I didn't make any cent off my first business. Grandma killed it.

Who knows, maybe I could have been the 1st rich and young black something.

1997 or 8, like a true m*^&&* I came back and started a farming business again, this time at my house (parents' house). It wasn't long enough till my mother killed it in the same fashion her mother did to my first. Mxm!!

I guess she got it from her mother!

Many years later, I also killed a lot of businesses.

I give credit to grandma and her daughter (momma) for not only infecting me with the spirit of killing businesses. But also never discouraging me from doing anything I wanted to do in life, and actually allowing such space. They gave me the money to buy those seeds.

I appreciate it. I am able to persist and move forward after a dead venture.

I thought it would be fun writing this post, I couldn't figure the moral of it. It is just a reminder of my love for entrepreneurship.

IMPORTANT LESSON BUSINESS PLANS FAIL TO TEACH: FINDING PENETRATIVE ADVANTAGES

The other day I was consulting a lady who wants to start a sort of high end clothing label for preteens, but as everyone – she doesn't have funds and is demoralized at the thought that it might be tough to get funding for her awesome business idea.

The reality is money isn't cheap. It is only smart for investors to backup projects which have some traction or leverage: Either the venture has produced some directional progress or the entrepreneur has some entrepreneurial experience.

No one is forced to finance anyone. I often hear aspiring entrepreneurs complain that getting funding is hard. The entitlement mentality can hold a person back.

She is worried about writing a proper business plan. Every day the thought of her not pursuing her clothing business pains her.

For a new entrepreneur, the worry should be about exploring possible simple angles to at least start the business however small the steps and despite of what she doesn't have.

She will realize her priority goal is not necessarily to get funding but to make the business work and mitigate risk.

A business plan is a tool required by banks to evaluate the risk of financing a business. It is like a questionnaire. However awakening it is in alerting the entrepreneur of important business concepts, it doesn't help one forge a penetrative angle thoughtful or mindful of the limited resources.

Now, when pursuing business, given resources might be limited and scare, one needs to figure a way to make it work inspite of. Business plans do not teach you how to do that.

This is the ethos of what the **EBC business model** in my book '**Forget The Business Plan Use This Short Model**' teaches. Business plans wont teach you an angle to make a business work given the 'have not's'.

I showed her she can start bit by bit.

- -

Her model is to make the clothes on order and on a week's turnaround. This is good and possible if she has a reliable CMT (Cut Make Trim manufacturer).

Firstly I asked her to list clothing items she would like to make, they were: jeans, shirts, caps, t-shirts and belts

I asked her to figure out which items are:

-   Easy for her to make and sell.
-   Hold higher value in consumer's eye than the others.
-   Easily strike attention to her brand
-   Price the buyers (parents) are willing to pay.

Belts and caps are easy to make or source. She can even buy readymade and brand. Embroidery is the cheapest as screen print requires setup costs per print run.

The idea is not to be fancy or wait for until one has the PERFECT resources. The idea is to find what is workable, get in the market with it and use the proceeds to finance the fancy stuff.

Jeans are of higher value. She discovered parents are liberal on their prices depending on how sharp the jeans are.

Well crafted jeans would strike attention. Caps also. Sharply branded t-shirts yes.

The limitation with on-order-made t-shirts is every single time she prints, a setup cost (R150 plus) is required, and it isn't justifiable for just one item.

The idea here was to find **penetrative advantage** products, i.e. one or two products which are easy for her to make, finance and sell. And holds higher value for the consumer and would easily cause a stir in the market thus exposing her infant brand.

Jeans and caps are products which might have that penetrative advantage in her case.

So, from thereon is for her to make samples of the products. It could be even be 2 of each. Dress her cute kid and take photos. Viva Instagram filters. Or even create a Pinterest board, then screen munch it to use as catalogue.

Then from thereon she markets the business and takes orders. The question would be where to find parents whom might have interest in her clothes but in bundles.

- The start is everyone she knows: friends, family, acquaintances etc.
- She can test her social media audience. If the clothes strike attention, the word to the right people will spread.
- Negotiate exhibition space at school activities where parents are invited.
- Depending how she feels about it, but if it were me – I would convince crèches (pay) to put the catalogues in the kids' backpacks.
- Introduce her brand to kid's blogs.

Nothing fancy. Interaction with the market will tell her where to improve and how to proceed.

It is about testing, without much capital outlay.

DATING ADVICE THAT CAN SAVE YOUR BUSINESS, FROM A NO GAME ENTREPRENEUR

While we were on a date, she posted on her Facebook: "On a date, he is boring. I hate guys who cannot make conversation. This is a regrettable waste of my Sunday, the worst eveeeeer."

I was a bore, I froze, and conversation wouldn't come. We were connected by a mutual lady friend, Thapelo.

The date was going wrong. To avert the silence, we both fiddled with our phones. That is how I came across her Facebook status.

"She is beautiful, single and looking", I heard; she was. She wanted a man who is doing not so bad and is also ambitious. "I'm ambitious. I fit the profile – why not give it a try?" I thought.

After the date I told my best friend Lesiba. "Don't worry mfana, clearly she doesn't know you well and never will", he said. Thanks chief.

To skip the foreplay: If the starter meals are not your forte – Jump to section **B**!

- -

A.
We got calls from customers complaining that the t-shirts they had bought from us were shrinking after washing.

It was 3+ weeks after Gabble Heights Clothing came out – and it was an immediate hit. We had sold a bunch of stock and produced +-100 units.

Tiisetso Maloma

Most people starting clothing brands buy promotional t-shirts, at around R20 a piece and screen-print them at about R30a tee. And they are in business.

Me and my partner Lesiba Lekagau loved clothes, Diesel more especially. We envisioned a brand which could compete with them and company.

For 2 years I researched about making clothes: pattern cutting, fabric, stitching etc. I even travelled as far as Durban (from Joburg) as it has a lot of fabric and manufacturing factories. Our t-shirts sold at R350.

The detail of every angle was meticulously thought out. We came up with the phrase 'gabble heights';2 words which were totally never used together before – we gave them a single meaning.

Our garments were tailor made with the finest burling fabric. This is the stuff high-end brands use (at that time).

We had our own font. Our very own f*#%*n font! Shout to out Bill Botes, he designed the font for us. When I tried to pay him for marvellous work he had done, he said "no." Thanks a lot Bill, I learned a lot from you.

Since our clothes were made from scratch and were printed with suede flock (It costs over R50 per t-shirt), to make one t-shirt cost us over R100. This is more than double compared to using promo tees and screen print.

The loss was a couple of thousands. Almost all our savings were put that order.

We discovered that our mistake was we didn't treat the fabric before handing it over to the CMT (Cut Make Trim) wehad outsourced. Treating it was supposed to be simple as putting the fabric in water overnight.

A 'yawn' to Lesiba and Tiisetso!

- -

B.

The date situation and gabble heights Clothing incident were hurtful.But I regret none.

However, to remedy business risks such as those of gabble heights, I apply an approach which Richard Branson calls 'protecting the downside.'Some might even call it the 'lean business approach.'

Because I am silly; below follows a 'going on a date' analogy to explain the concept.

Do not argue – Take it as I say it in order to understand.

Say you are a single guy and looking for a somewhat serious relationship.

You are in the market, browsing and surveying at a couple of opportunities (potential girlfriend). There are 3 ladies you have an interest in.

To try each, you are thinking a date.

Let's say a date costs R500. So for 3 dates it will be R1500. You can't take them out at once unless you are the Spinach King, I mean the Sushi King. The Sushi King says he is retired from dating an army of women (at the same damn time with their knowledge).

R1500's weight is relative to different people. To some it's expensive, to some not and others- fair. Some ladies seeing this are saying "sies that is so cheap and insulting Tiisetso."

The final goal is to get a girlfriend. Think of the dates as market exploration. If there is an option to cut down market exploration costs, it is a smart choice.

Who told you a dinner date is the best market exploration. You can do a coffee date (Did you know that? There are always options). Why immerse yourself under the pressure of being interesting and with a hefty bill at the same time?

Let's say a coffee date will cost R150 each. So, on separate dates with 3 women, it would be R450.

To apply the 'lean dating approach,' rather ask each out to a coffee date. Limit your time so you are not thought of as a cheap and easily available commodity; say to them you would liketo do coffee in the week for an hour or so. It is a small ask, I am sure they would oblige.

Using a lean dating approach to discover who you like better from the 3will cost you R450 with a coffee date (versus R1500 with a dinner date).

Coffee date = R1050 saving. Booooom!!

Then after, you would know whom you like better. Then you can take that one on a R500 date.

In total, with a lean approach, it costs R450 (3 coffee dates) plus R500 (single date with the one you like better) for a dinner date. Equals R950.

If you did dinner for the first 3 dates, you would have spent another R500 or more on a second date with the one you like better. That's like R2000 + to explore possible girlfriends (versus R950).

--

Even in business, don't go all out at first.

Ambition and conventional thinking sometimes lead us to spend drastically without weighing leaneroptions.

Protecting your downside is lowering possible losses. Entrepreneurship is risky anyway. You are trying to minimize the risk of exploring that particular business, by launching and testing it in different small inexpensive stages.

In the case of gabble heights, ifI had to do it again, I wouldn't print 100 t-shirts. I would do 20 just to test, and not pump almost all my savings into a venture – especially a business I am totally new to. The market will help me on how to proceed.

--

Unlike while on dates, the beauty of business is you can go home and think about. If not, it is a casino like gamble. Maybe you are being crooked.

Actually, she as well didn't have conversation.

There is no shame in walking away with shame, I tell myself.

THE COMPASSION OF A BUSINESS MODEL

Keep going. This is the generally given advice on tackling and choke-slamming doubt, and the feeling of ineptness that creeps in on one, when one's executed actions towards a goal aren't proving fruitful.

I did this with gabble heights Clothing, I even paused/abandoned other business pursuits to zone my **focus** on one unit of enterprise. Months went by; sales weren't that great or even improving. Other income opportunities were lost of course, now came in the daunting and depressing feeling of not affording one's self: shelter, food and R45.00 for a six pack of Windhoek beer.

Mentally I wasn't ok, physically I was doing well (exercise is good for the mind), but I was 'keep going'.

Let me jump to the message at topic, I will finish this later, of course in this post.

- -

The realization

Yes startup capital is vital for new businesses, but one of the main factors limiting new and aspiring entrepreneurs is lack of foresight in creating and innovating their products to meet/produce value and efficiency for the consumer.

Below are few problems new entrepreneurs meet.

Young entrepreneurs see inability to secure funding as a dream killing block, whereas there are innovative bootstrapping ways to explore.

Young entrepreneurs have difficulty in programming their products to meet consumer value. We are focused on being entrepreneurs; entrepreneurship is about getting a kick out of the consumer, but not being consumed to self.

Young entrepreneurs have difficulty in relating (marketing) their product to potential consumers. It's important to make consumers understand the value one's our products can play in their lives. If still they don't understand, refresh your product relation (marketing), and if still, innovate the product. So on and so forth, until they buy.

Difficulty marking possible buyers and branding their products accordingly to meet the afore mentioned. Its expensive and such a long shot to market to everyone initially, zone in on who is likely to buy the quickest. That's cash flow to survive.

The answer: definition of a business model

A business model takes in kind:

A product designed with the consumer's satisfaction in mind.

A product to serve value and efficiency to the consumer, thus rendering a difference to the perspective consumer, who then shows appreciation for the difference by committing their money on the product.

Establishing efficient (for the consumer) consumption points, or rather efficient distribution channels, which make it easy for the consumer to acquire the product.

 The marketing process is a stage where the entrepreneur relates the value and usability of the product to society.

But first, categorizing which sectors/people/class/sub-cultures might buy the product, then prioritizing them on who is likely to buy the quickest.

Then approaching the prospects in a manner affordable to the entrepreneur and effective in getting the prospective consumer attention.

After a short sabbatical and assessment, of me and the world. The fault wasn't me not managing to 'keep going'. Our products were good, but our marketing and distribution weren't zoned in, they weren't focused. These 2

Tiisetso Maloma

activities (marketing and distribution) were eating our cash reserves faster than we could afford.

Marketing has to engage the target market in a sense that it brings in sales, enough sales to afford the marketing. In a bootstrapping sense, the sales have to be almost immediate. Otherwise you die, like we did.

Our marketing was scattered in many places at once, it was expensive: Sekhukhune, Johannesburg, Pretoria, Durban and Polokwane. By the time we tried to negotiate with it as to what was wrong, we were financially bust, the scattered marketing ate our cash reserves. Had we zoned in one area, we would have been sustainable, then leveraging that to grow further into other areas. Even the distribution was straining and expensive.

For a startup, when marketing is focused on a certain area firstly, it's easier to assess the impact (marketing to sales). Easier to make changes quickly, the distribution as well is easier, as probably you frequent that particular area.

To grow, when that area is conquered, you move to the next, conquer it and then to the next. Cash flow is survival.

We decided to close gabble heights Clothing, or rather put it on pause. Lesson well learned, and has proved very useful on other ventures we have moved on to. At least bread gets to sit with us when we have breakfast, and financially I'm recovering (can now afford 6 pack Windhoek beer, sometimes).

The decision (to close gabble heights) wasn't easy, but I got to make up with sanity (insanity is...). Before deciding to close the business, I was clueless on how to improve things. The break helped me understand and seek: what went wrong, what to do to refinance the business, ask advice and importantly, how I was going to afford myself as I was terribly broke.

Gabble heights Clothing will be back, this time in a different way, I hope this move will shock people. Sometimes, you can't 'keep going' the same way.

Challenges are not won by 'keep going' but by creative solutions, thinking outside the box and reassessment.

ARE YOU UN-NETWORKING ?

Networking is supposed t be a maneuver wherein one links with people in one way or another; with the intention of deriving or attracting future value, through putting out information which might benefit them-people, even if you don't directly gain. This is hard for me to explain, but I trust you get the gist of what networking is.

I'm becoming less of a terrible networker. Maybe it's because I know how I add value to processes, businesses or people. So when you ask me what I do, I just shout how I help out where I help out.

At The Hookup Dinner a while ago (it's a networking event for entrepreneurs ok), I heard the networking queen (Helen Nicholson) say, when you tell people of what you do, say something like: I specialize in helping businesses achieve one two three. Not her exact words, but you catch my drift. This way of explaining exudes trust, and is welcoming, and leaves room for further conversation.

Un-networking

This is something perhaps a lot us of do unaware. We tarnish the value we possibly possess/portray, or chances of attaining any value.

How?

At some point in your life, you have met a guy who works at, example - a clothing shop. This chap can get you (right word is steal) clothes at discounted prices, from his employer's shop, but without their knowledge. He even boasts about it. The whole hood knows about him.

This fella's network keeps growing, more and more people want to know him. I guess most of us are crooks; we always want stuff at bootleg prices. Actually who is better: those who want stuff at bootleg prices or those who knowingly buy knock-offs (counterfeit).

As the fellow boasts about what he does, he gets famous (notorious bastard), his network grows through not even just his efforts, but of others (referrals are important).

The fellow above is un-networking himself. If you hear of a job opening at a shop owned by one of your friend or associate, honestly - would you recommend this thieving chap? Probably not! If yes, then you are bad for your friend's (the shop owner) network.

Are you this guy? Were you ever this guy? I've been the guy that claims to know this guy. And I was lying; I just wanted to be cool.

Unaware, we always network some sort of value. Either this value is working for us or against us.

The basic and best thing for us is to decide on a meaningful journey that has long term beneficial value for our careers. We shouldn't be known as the thieving and dubious fella.

Rather be known as the shop salesman who is good at his job. It's not quick cash probably, but if you invest in developing the kind of value you can add to the world, then your career path will be greener and very wealthy.

I trust you know a good graphic designer, the operative word being 'good'. When you refer this good graphic designer to someone else, you mention a 'good' graphic designer'.

Be the 'good' graphic designer who practices hard to be good, so people can refer you to their networks as 'good'.

When you un-network yourself, no one wants to lift you higher, they want you to remain where you are so they can benefit from you only in that one way. They actually want you to remain as their dog, not dawg.

Of course these people would want you to grow into premium shops, so you can steal premium brands for them, but as long as its shops not owned by anyone they care about.

Tiisetso Maloma

They won't promote you into their network. They want you to remain in the next network so they can benefit from you but at the same time make sure you don't contaminate their precious networks.

THE UNDERWORLD OF STARTUP ENTREPRENEURS | CHRONICLES OF A STRUGGLING (SUCCEEDING) ENTREPRENEURS

The fridge was empty. I swore to myself that the following day I would hustle like I never did before. I don't know why but the implication of an empty fridge hurts more than not eating the actual food. This can't be 3rd world problems, can it? Things got better as they always do. Months later I was back in a similar situation of having a horribly empty refrigerator. My life has had a rollercoaster of these episodes.

I must do some shit to rid my life of such low points forever. Points which make none believers not understand why folks like me sacrifice to push what is called a "dream".

On the other hand, like the rest of society, I don't like to keep it real. It is like I paint a champagne life with a cheap BIC pen.

You know what kind of society we are? We are a country of people who when they give directions dish out driving directions. We know very well not everyone has or can have a car. For good's sake we are labelled a developing world, a 3rd world country. Poverty is rife. Our unemployment can drown Noah's Ark.

Anyway, we don't care. Driving directions are the order of the day. Even job interviews, conferences and other event shapes events give driving directions. I guess keeping out public transport directions assumes and maintains prestige.

Tiisetso Maloma

I wanted to co-write this article with a friend but he refused as he doesn't want to be construed as a "loser". He is doing well; I don't know why he is petrified of sharing some of these things he bluntly knows entrepreneurs go through – as he himself has had a share of. I am going to quote him below.

Like the rest of society, him – me – you – us – everyone, are bias in projecting success. Only he winning strokes make it publicly.

I heard someone say "why does X put himself through this shitty hustling lifestyle even though he has a degree".

Entrepreneurship is tough. It takes you through several moments of insanity. The things entrepreneurs sacrifice to achieve their uncertain ambitions is UNBELIEVABLE. But this article isn't about why people choose entrepreneurship.

There is a good article published by The Economist titled "Instead of romanticising entrepreneurs people should understand how hard their lives can be". You should check it.

What will follow is the truth. If you are an entrepreneur this is the gospel. It is the underworld of startup entrepreneurship.

Aspiring entrepreneurs, ahead there is these, maybe.

Obviously some of these happened to be me, but not all unfortunately. I borrowed some. At least I have struggle credentials. I am writing this stuff because I hope it will firstly humour you. Secondly, this sh*t happens, to get to point B – sometimes ideals have to be skipped. When such is forewarned and when it actually occurs, it humours. And when it is told, it is humour. "Comedy is tragedy plus time", even google is unsure who said this, but it must have been some comedian as the legend goes.

- I saw a guy at a restaurant in Pretoria wearing a green suit. The following day I saw him at a conference in Sandton with the same suit. In my head I gave him a nod and said "right on brother, do your thing. Only respect". And the following week I saw him again with the same suit. I am kidding on the third encounter.
- Thanks to Lesiba for sponsoring over 70% of that day's lunch at Fish and Chips. Lunch for 3.
- Killing time by playing with kids, because you can't afford to go anyway or borrow the acquaintance of a lady.
- Walking for a 2.5 km to a meeting. Or 4 km. Or more.
- Waking up to do best with the R10 airtime you have to push progress. Luckily, no, by God's Grace a friend buys you R20 airtime.
- A quote from that friend mine. I stole it from our group chats: "I wake up today Monday 28 June very broke, haven't being this broke in a long time, though in a life on an entrepreneur one has been through these moments a lot of times but one should never get used to it. Nonetheless I woke up with one plan in mind: chase as many people as I can for appointments with the R20 airtime that I put on this phone. You know to keep every call to 2 minutes at least and get that person's email address. That is what we call maximising resources, Hustlers Verse 1. To all entrepreneurs know one thing: some days will be hard than others but always be persistent on your journey. Hustle hard".
- Abusing your Blackberry keyboard to send multiple emails because you are out of data bundles on your laptop.
- Computer hijacking because you don't have one, i.e. using someone's laptop when they are on a break.
- Walking distances, again. And again.
- The easy part is moving back home because you cannot afford yourself anymore. If you are currently going through this, tears won't help you.

- The harder one is moving in with friends. Especially if you are a 'caring caring' person who wholly respects other people's space. I don't understand some people who can borrow someone's space and not keep it clean like their hosts.
- Revisiting old roll on bottles as you've just totally exhausted the current one. No money for news ones.
- Calling your mom as a last option and asking for money to get to your meeting. It is a potential meeting; but you know it could go either way.
- Cancelling a meeting as you don't have funds.
- Walking distances in the sun. You need lots of sunglass pairs if you are an entrepreneur.
- Walking 2.9 km from Sunninghill to Woodmead as you took the wrong taxi. Misdirection boss.
- Wanting to lick someone for giving you R10 to buy airtime.
- **PLEASE SHARE YOUR STORIES IN THE COMMENTS OR EMAIL THEM TO ME. I WILL ADD THEM TO THE ARTICLE.**

Hang in there, don't worry. You are going to win.

Chris Gardner as we saw in that movie "The Pursuit of Happiness" went through some testing times. One of my favourite scenes was when he gladly, but reluctant inside, lent his boss his last dollar bill to pay off a taxi. The boss assumed a dollar bill isn't much for a guy in a nice suit like Chris.

Chris Gardner faked it.

The number one enemy in South Africa for the youth (and I am only saying this to stress a point; I am not a doctored social scientist whatsoever) is maintaining an assumed class. Twitter is one of the barometers for this fallacious class. The solution lies with the individual. Know the world likes to pretend ideals, know your situation and do venture into your goals – even if it upsets class ideals. Sometimes, don't be afraid to fake it.

2 LESSONS FROM HOW SOUTH AFRICAN TOWNSHIP BUSINESSES ARE STARTED AND GROWN

I was giving a talk a few weekends ago at an Inspiring Women event. I spoke of the 'importance of starting small in business. One of the examples I related was on what can be learned from how township businesses are started.

There are a number of reasons someone in the township starts a business. The exemplary world view is a mother starting a business out of the need or desperation to feed one's family. Be it as it may, 'passion to enterprise' is fast overweighing the desperation to make ends meet. People are being exposed on how to offer great value even when in a dire situation.

Township business is sometimes looked down on, but it practices brilliant concepts which anyone can use to start and grow their business. However they the township businesses forget to grow and progress further on the very principles.

After the talk, 2 groups of people came to me asking further on the teachings of township business. They found the concept very enlightening and helpful.

So here I borrowed few words from my free booklet 'Township Biz Fastrack' which I co-authored with www.spazanews.co.za.

Normally when township businesses are started, the startup products are either strategic or 'passion products'.

What I mean by strategic is, the business owner realises there is a gap in his surrounding market. It could be he/she believes he can sell colder soft drinks than the nearest shop or that his neighbours travel far to get soft drinks.

By neighbours, I mean it in an African sense, LOL, not neighbour in the proximity sense.

A passion product is, for example: the lady starting the business could be good in making artchar or baking – so she decides to enterprise on the skill. Normally when people are passionate about something, they make sure it's good. They have an advantageous edge on regular competition.

Ok, how they would start is, they would start with smaller quanties of stock, then add more with the proceeds to grow the business. In modern entrepreneurship definitions, this is called **bootstrapping.** The business is grown by funding its own growth. Isn't this awesome, it is less risk on own funds.

Ever asked the new spaza shop down your street to sell airtime or anything you need which they don't stock? This is it, customers will then advise the shop owner/keeper who only sells soft drinks or artchar to add something that would of convenience to them. This is called **validation.**

It is an easy transaction, customers are advising what to stock and they will buy.

The lessons:

1. **If you start small, you learn more with minimal investment**. Of course we know of a timer who got their pension money and invested it all into something he calls a hotel but things don't quiet work out. So they lost out big as they went in big.
2. **The experience which you gather informs you of where to re-invest your proceeds and invest your savings** – WISELY.

So, there is hope for even businesses which are started out of desperation to feed one's self or family. Validation and bootstrapping are important to grow any business.

HOW TO GET AND KEEP A MENTOR: WHY NOBODY WANTS YOUR COFFEE OFFER

I can't recall how many times but I did propose to buy coffee to people I wanted mentorship from.

A mentor is someone more prominent than me, right? How the hell do I suppose I will attract Brian Joffe to meet me all because I offered to buy him coffee.

He can afford way more than his own coffee and can only drink so much. I am sure he has coffee invites from Zimbabwe to Zanzibar.

Had inviting people out for coffee been that intriguing, I would have invited Azania many times. How I wish.

A mentor is important in that they can save you from making stupid mistakes and loses, and introduce you to prospective clients.

- -

How to get a mentor

I often get mentorship requests via email or social media. Most of those never go anywhere.

I do have mentors. Real and virtual. Virtual could mean reading Richard Branson's biography, reading Marc Cuban's blog or following Lebo Gunguluza's story.

The thing about mentorship is it isn't formal. What happens after you ask someone to mentor you? You can't nag them with meetings and calls all week. A relationship based on you always needing never lasts. It runs out of steam. The ever needed party gets bored.

35

Tiisetso Maloma

Let me give an example of one my now mentors, Bra Noel Ndlhvu of Spaza News. I made a blind call to him, briefed him of a free book I am was writing and asked for his articles to be included.

It pleased him that someone is interested in his articles and wants to in essence advertise them further. It gave or aroused a good emotion in him.

Now and then he and I meet; I listen to what he is working on, help or advice how I can. In exchange, he also gives me a whole lot of advice.

You see, he's is more experienced than me in business, but still I try offer him something. So the relationship doesn't get boring (one sided).

Some steps to get a mentor:

- Identify them.
- Be interested in what they have done.
- Introduce yourself.
- Inquire from them about the particular interest you have of them.
- Figure out what they are working on.
- Become useful and think of ways you can help out (for free).

I have had good mentors. Some I lost contact with and some I suspect hate my guts, for reasons I cannot write about (or yet). "Some mentors will eventually hate you", someone said.

STRATEGY ON FORMULATING AN APPROACH TO THE PRICE QUOTING STAGE

The quoting process needs to be afforded a psychological strategy and continuous training. It should not be as easy as hiring someone, giving them cubicle, phone, email address and a chair.

Its one thing when people see your company's awesome and attractive advertisement, and when they do call in to enquire.

Sit down with the whole of your team regularly (especially marketing and product development/innovation); discuss how the quotation process should go to catch sales. It's in understanding what your product can do versus what the prospective customer wants to achieve. Business is about offering value which clients use to leverage their business dealings, not ripping people off.

Respect and courtesy are intertwined with business, kindred spirits as some say. Being courteous gives assurance to prospective clients as to why they should stay with you. It humbles them to your brand.

Training. Whoever handles the quotation process, after being part of the discussion mentioned above, has to understand your company and its product offerings. Their duty sounds easy as just capturing what marketing (even word of mouth) has caught, but it's totally delicate. The fish brings itself to their attention; all they have to do in not scare them away but give a good impression of the company.

They are the ones that execute what is being preached in this post, amen.

As the manager, you have to make sure they are humble to: respect and courtesy (following up and updating enquirers).

Points to note:

Nice and short welcoming greetings: "...this is Tiisetso at your assistance".

Listen to what they need, and for what they are going to use it for. Don't force it out of them though; it might be for discreet purposes.

Confirm what they just said they need.

You are at service here, get their contact number first, and then email address, so that you can email them what you require in order to prepare a quotation. Ask them if they are ok to listen to the requirements over the phone.

The trick is not to scare them off by requesting too much detail at first. Avoid giving them anything that they could procrastinate over, if possible.

Travelling to clients. It depends on how much you can make from each sale. Evaluate your company's ability against the possibilities. Maybe try it on a couple of clients, as a test.

Help them to use your company's product offering effectively to match their need/use. This is how you keep them close; this is how you stay in their mind as a good supplier/service-provider, this way they will come back and refer others.

They need a service rendered, not for you to rip them by selling them more than they need.

Formulated training. Make the quoting stage as part of your business model; it has to be documented in some form of a training manual. For each learning point, give a reason as to why.

YOUR QUOTATION PROCESS CAN COST YOU POTENTIAL CLIENTS

Being in the clothing industry, it involves ever searching for new, cheaper and better suppliers. We always experience bad service in this regard.

There we are looking for printing quotations. Phoning and emailing printers, in some instances visiting their offices. These all costs money.

What do we get? Some of these entities don't even respond to our emails or return calls. We end up having to be the one's making follow ups. Us the potential clients begging for quotations!

What to do not to get business

Not respond to emails

Please respond to your emails. If you do not understand the contents of an email, give the potential client a call.

Not indicate response time

It is best to give an indication of when you will furnish the potential client a quotation. If you don't, the client could bug you with follow-up calls and end up getting annoyed with your uncertainty.

Unfriendly reception

Your reception or whoever is responsible for preparing quotations should nicely and properly brief inquirers of what is needed to furnish a quotation.

No communicating processes

It is possible that a client's query won't get replied to in time. If that is the case, inform them beforehand.

HOW I OVERCAME BEING A BAD NETWORKER

I'm just not a good networker. I envy those guys who have the skill to speak to just anyone, like my good friend Paseka Kalaku. I suck at introducing myself to lots of people at an event. What is to follow is how a mediocre networker like me manages to more than just mange at networking.

The other night I was in Robebank, I bumped into a good guy by the name Suede. This dude is a great connector. After greeting him I wondered why I felt gratitude towards him. I remembered that he once referred my then clothing label 'gabble heights' to participate in an African Fashion International event, without him knowing me personally then. The mileage from that event was awesome.

I guess Maya Angelou was right when she said: "I've learned that people will forget what you said, people will forget what you did, but people will never forget how you made them feel."

He added value to me and I'm forever grateful, and I'm sure in the future I can add value to him too.

With having the concept of adding value in mind, let's go to the next part...
- - -

I'm sure you are going to attend a lot of networking events this year, with the aim of attracting good contacts. And I'm sure in the past or still now you collect a lot of business cards there – 7 to 10 or more, right?

When you get home you do email these folks, just to say hi or whatever. How many do reply? Not a lot a right? All that effort! It hurts.

A mentor of mine keeps saying you know you have made it when you don't reply to all emails. I guess he is talking about mails from guys like me.

41

Tiisetso Maloma

It's ok. Here is something that I do and is working well for me in growing my network. I don't make it a point to collect a lot of business cards or meet everyone at an event, 5 cards are ok. I make it a point to get into a bit detailed conversations with these 5 people.

A good conversation is one where you are listening, asking questions, probing and, giving advice if suitable. Everyone likes to talk about themselves. So that's easy.

When I get home, I look at each card and think who I can link this person with - so they both can benefit from each other or maybe even do business together. I don't have to gain financially. Or I try helping them get a solution to their challenge which they told me of at the event.

So, the best way I grow my network is I try to add value to whoever I invite in it. These people will know me as a person of value, and will refer me to others as a person with value. The best business I enjoy is referral business.

I have noticed that some of the best relationships I enjoy are those where I added a bit of value, without it being asked for. And, some good people I lost, are those whom I persistently only took from.

I don't need to introduce myself to 100 people at one event; I just have to add value to my current network and think creatively of how to add value to whoever I want to invite in it.

Once you add value to someone, they will ever feel gratitude towards you.

USING YOUR PASSION TO KILL PROCRASTINATION

Hard work is procrastinated but fun work is done now.

Finding the passion

I take it you are determined in whatever field you are in and also aspire to achieve a certain career goal.

And we are all passionate about something. But we can agree that procrastination hits us when we try to action our passions. Anything before taking the first step towards achieving a goal is a mere dream, a mere fantasy.

Thinking of your dreams brings about this joyful sensation. I'm sure achieving the actual dream would bring riveting joy than the fantasy of living the dream. This riveting joy is fulfilment and happiness, as a benchmark can be pointed and quantified.

Believe me you, merely dreaming and not doing anything to fulfil the fantasy will bring about envy; envy of those that are living their dreams and envy of living your dream. This envy then turns into unhappiness.

This unhappiness is brought about by lack of ambition and motivation to take the first step. No one to blame but yourself.

I hope this envy burns and chokes you, brings you so much unhappiness until you cant live with it, until you want to die, until you decide to do something about it. I'm kidding.

Here is a trick I use whenever procrastination visits my rich soul.

Look, if you take a step towards your goal, it means you closer than before.

Now dwell and linger on the thought of getting closer to your dreams through action. It would be joy right, knowing you are getting closer to your dreams? You would want to work harder, so that you get closer and closer! The closer, the extreme the happiness!

We can now attach happiness to the act of executing dreams. Therefore, since dreaming brings a bit of joy, taking action on the dreams also brings joy and happiness as you know you are getting closer to achieving the dream. And definitely achieving the dream is happiness and fulfilment.

Therefore, for passion to render any joy to you, you have to action it.

For your passion to render joy to you, you have to take calculated action/s to achieving the goal of that passion.

Established here now is that procrastination is the enemy of achieving your passion, it lives in deterring your action spirit.

Killing procrastination

I'm living my dreams, which is going after my dreams. Most times I dread to complete my 'to-do-list', like you. I give all sorts reasonable reasons as to why. The best one is, adding more work to tomorrow's 'to-do-list'. Needless to say that I never complete all of tomorrow's to do list, which gets carried over to the following day.

 "Hard work is procrastinated but fun work is done now".

Procrastination is that enemy which says to you, don't do this important task of achieving your dreams now, but do it later.

You kill procrastination by dwelling on the thought that through action, your dreams are closer to being realised.

Multitasking

Why do you multitask. Multitasking produces worry, as you are doing this and this at the same time, there you are worrying that you won't do that. So much unnecessary strain on your brain, no peace of mind.

As an entrepreneur (for example), what matters is money : i.e. doing what brings in money. Money is not brought by refining and updating your business plan (if you are not trying to get funding), it is brought by connecting with the outside world, making contact, relating your offerings to prospective clients and checking up on your old clients.

This is what I call keeping **main things main**, working the main things then down. That's taking care of business baby.

Answering the problem of multitasking. Focus on a single task, as you are more creative and focused that way. Finish that task then move to the next. Single-tasking helps you give your full clinical attention to a task. I'm not saying take your time completing a task; assign a time frame to complete whatever task, as other things still have to be done too. But still it must be work you would be proud of. This acumen develops through practice; you get better through practice.

The best way to kill procrastination is to get on and do the job without thinking of it. Take a sit at your desk, decide which task is of money making priority, the do it. A cool tip would be to schedule a completion time for each task.

But last week procrastination violated me. Over the weekend as I rested, I realised it was telling me I need to innovate my projects further, as they were starting to be boring. Excitement keeps you going.

HOW TO SURRENDER LIKE MONIQUE BINGHAM

Monique said to me, "thank you baby...". I replied "thank you my love" in silence. You might be thinking I am cold for not returning her appreciation.

- -

Lets' trace <u>Monique Bingham</u>'s songs up till <u>'Take Me to My Love' with Ralf Gum.</u>

Easily, I think of her 2000 track with Blue 6 – <u>'Pure'</u>. <u>'We Had a Thing'</u> with Abstract Truth in 1998. Or <u>'poor people'</u> in 2008.

We can even jump to <u>'Pride'</u> with DJ Pepsi in 2012.

A lot of South Africans (me included) did not connect Monique's old songs and recent songs to the same person. I do hope this admission does not tarnish my house head credentials. I can hear some <u>house heads</u> going "only you Shog – we knew it was the same person". The Shog was/is my DJ name if you didn't know.

You know how <u>music heads</u> can be.

The reason we were not able to trace her is, I think, she surrenders to each of her songs. She allows herself to get lost in each and every one of them; hence we weren't able to trace her.

It is like she first meditates to a song before recording so to be one with it and inside of it when she sings it out. When she delivers it, it is like she is assigned to sing it like it is meant to feel, not how her singing personality is. It is like she does not sing as Monique Bingham but as a soul specially contracted to express that one song.

There are many signers whose method is first their singing personality and thereafter comes the music. For some it works and others not so much.

I hold Stimela to high regard. I think they are in the same greatness box as The Beatles. Their song writing ability is intensely informed and timelessly relevant. The point I want to make is Stimela and The Beatles don't sing with the same precision as your singers like Donny Hathaway and Eddie Levert. But they tap toe to toe with them with equal amount of talent and greatness.

Tiisetso Maloma

I feel Stimela and The Beatles surrender to songs. It is like they are character singers in their own music. I love Stimela.

Fela Kuti isn't a precision singer but he can take you there musically than your Idols winning singers.

- -

There are so many opportunities and challenges circling in front of me right now. Of course I am doing everything in my power not to let the opportunities slip.

But for some reason I have surrendered to 2 things separately: 'working hard' and 'tomorrow taking care of itself'. Tomorrow I will do whatever needs to done to the best of my abilities. I will stay away from the anxiety and consciousness that some things might not go as I wish them to, no matter how hard I try. I am at peace with whatever I am doing at this moment and whatever I will do tomorrow. Right now I am writing this article.

I will be like Monique Bingham; I will surrender to each task I will be performing, then the next one, the other and other.

- -

I first tweeted her "It's like @moniquebingham meditates for her songs so to get lost in each. Each is like a diff world. I call it method singing #goodmusic"

Then she replied and said "thank u baby tryin to zone out to zone in right now #writersblock"

Top | Live | Accounts | Photos | Videos | More options ∨

monique bingham @moniquebingham · 2 Jun 2015
thank u baby tryin to zone out to zone in right now #writersblock

> **pre-order #TAEbook** @TiisetsoMaloma
> It's like @moniquebingham meditates for her songs so to get lost in each.
> Each is like a diff world. I call it method singing #goodmusic

1   4

THE REASONS WHY PEOPLE DO NOT WANT YOU TO FOLLOW YOUR DREAMS

I am on a blogging marathon promoting of my upcoming 3ʳᵈ book (28 October 2015), The Anxious Entrepreneur. Pre-order it at up to 40% discount.

People like to dig and analyse people's background affairs.

A homeboy was saying to me I wouldn't be pursuing entrepreneurship had my parents not been doing ok. He meant, given otherwise, I would have been forced to take a job to keep things going in the family.

It got me thinking of how fortunate I am.

He has a good job and a family of his own. He badly wants to pursue a business interest of his.

People look at their situations; they find what seemingly impedes them from pursuing their dreams. When they talk to you, the darer, about dreams and stuff, they attack what **SEEMS** to be enabling you to do what you do.

Strictly looking at what disables them will never enable them.

People want you to settle for normal and safety nets like they have. They want to feel good about settling and want to extend that colony by discouraging others. You are a disruption, so they have to counter you. You remind them of what they wish they could do.

- -

I have a family member who used to push me to get a job. Today he has turned to entrepreneurship, after 20 or so years of employment. I am 28. I love him still.

Tiisetso Maloma
I guess prior to turning to entrepreneurship full time, he was projecting his fears onto me.

- -

Your mom, the one who loves you to bits, could wish you to stop dreaming of pursuing dreams or stop chasing them if you are already.

In the start of a dream, it is rough. Your mom cannot stomach seeing you struggle because she loves you too much.

She probably prefers something safe for you, so you could be like other kids.

- -

Reasons Why People Want You To Settle For Normal
- You remind them of the dreams they punked out of.
- The want to project their fears onto you.
- They love you.

FOUR WAYS FOR ENTREPRENEURS TO DEFUSE ANXIETY

These points are extracted from my upcoming book The Anxious Entrepreneur.

It was at about 3:35 pm. I felt I was about to faint or have a panic attack. The day was not going well. Over and above, I was overly tired.

It had been weeks since I had any 'win'. Therefore I needed to hustle people on the phone even if it was 4:00 pm. I was desperate. For goodness' sake, that time is around knock off time. A business pitch is the last thing they would want to hear.

A rejection email had heightened the panic. All these triggered my mind to think I have no hope: immediately, I time travelled in the past and the future. I saw no advantage of what my past has brought to today and I saw no light in my future.

Below is what I do to counter such episodes.

1. Start the day with personal achievement activities
I start my day at 5 am with what appeals to my being and interest. I write articles for my blog or to a book until 6:30 am.

This signals my subconscious that I have fulfilled a self actualising activity. Throughout the day, I become somewhat robust to knocks.

My other interests are reading and running. Before writing, I read a few pages from books I like so to activate my literature mood. "Every morning I wake up and run away", said a certain soccer player. I also run away jogging in the morning at about 8am.

2. Work on 'business potential' tasks early on and for a fixed time

I find the mornings to be a good space to type out business pitch emails. The previous day, I would have made calls and got email addresses.

This is after I have written but before I go jogging: 6:45 to 8 am.

After my jog, I feel I have done enough to win the day. I am fulfilled throughout. The day could follow no particular pattern; I do what needs to be done.

Pitching business all day long is the right ingredient to send entrepreneurs to the highest anxiety hills. I prefer to do it for a fixed period. This makes sure I am effective.

3. Escape frustration tasks

I believe on that day, the tasks I was doing weren't directed by a good sense of business value but frustration and desperation. There I was thinking I am adding points to my 'working hard' score-card.

The pitches I was making didn't thoroughly consider fair value-add to those I was pitching. I just wanted to win. I was being a nuisance and spam.

So when I feel like I am being desperate to win, I take a break from work so to zone out from the anxiety.

4. Other people's energies

Whenever I feel close to being overly desperate to win, I know it might be all about 'me me me'.

I read somewhere that Shark Tank's - Robert Harjavec was saved from his depression and suicidal thoughts by volunteering at a soup kitchen.

He got severely depressed after his marriage ended. He turned to his pastor who advised him to give his time at the shelter.

There is this amazing and relinquishing energy which transmutes back to us when we give and help out.

- -

I went to sleep. I played the movie 300 so it can get me to doze off. I am a comedy guy and action movies usually make me sleep. I tend to use them as sleeping pills.

When I woke up, I was feeling better. I even played Donny Hathaway's rendition of 'To be Young, Gifted and Black'. It always soothes me. Always! Later on, I checked my emails and I had new business...

HOW TO WIN PEOPLE OVER IN BUSINESS THROUGH PICKUP ARTIST PATTERNS

Quick one: Who here was ashamed of any of their body features back in primary or high school, and what was it?

I was chubby and had an ass at the start of my high school. I remember I would tuck-in loose so as to conceal it. Tucking in was strictly enforced at Bopedi Bapedi. I later realised newbies listen to everything they are told. Of course you should adhere to all codes at school.

As high school progressed, the chubbiness was fading off, but the ass was taking its time.

- -

In tertiary, I was fascinated by the VHI TV series 'The Pickup Artist'. It was pickup artists teaching guys who couldn't approach girls of routines on how to do it. It captivated me greatly.

Sometime after I read 'The Game: Penetrating the Secret Society of Pickup Artists' by Neil Strauss.

Neil's book made me pay attention to social cues – which I never did before.

Being an entrepreneur, I realise approaches used by pickup artists can be of effect to business and career social dynamics.

In business or any career, like pickup artists' routines aim to achieve, you want people to:

(1). Open up to you and engage you
(2). Be comfortable with you
(3). See you as a person of value
(4). Like you
(5). Trust you

(6). Do business with you

- -

I am not a natural at some of these, especially walking up to people and introducing myself. I keep working on them.

Some things you have naturally and others you learn. If you aren't a natural conservationist, you can learn from those who have broken down the art of conversation.

Pickup artists have broken down female social dynamics (and males), developed tactics to infiltrate and draw attraction. Each tactic is tested to be valid.

They are often, rightfully and wrongfully criticised. This article doesn't deal with that; it is about connecting their patterns to business networking... Ladies and gents, in other news, we have a female seduction expert in South Africa, mme Mandisa O Mahlobo.

1. Open up to you and engage you

Here are two (mutually inclusive) ways to achieve this:

- Drawing attention and engagement
- Approaching indirectly

Draw attention and engagement

A normal gent like me would just say "hi" to a lady and hope she offers her undivided attention. We all know a 'hi' seldom succeeds. Women are used to replying back with a 'hi' - head set on their destination and walk off.

A pickup artist would first **say something that really draws the engagement of a woman's attention**: "excuse me, can I get your opinion on something". It draws attention. He continues "I need a lady's opinion. A lady friend of mine is struggling to decide if she should request her new boyfriend to remove pictures of his ex from his Facebook account. He doesn't upload pictures much, so the recent pics on his feed are of him and the ex being all cosy".

All this is meant to draw attention and engagement.

Ever felt a person just tricked you into a conversation? I have. They would start by mentioning a thing I did or somewhere I was with certain people. Silly me I am quickly drawn into the conversation and elaborating further. Sometime later they have steered the conversation into something they are doing or need. Slick m*^^.

They have just suckered my **attention and engagement.**

Approaching indirectly: Small talk doesn't necessarily have to be conscious, but has to be done

When Average Frustrated Chumps like us approach a girl, we consciously are direct in what we want from her. It starts from a 'hi' and immediately we seek her demographics: her name, where she stays, what she does for a living, contacts etc.

This approach is too direct and all about what we want to achieve. **It does not have an inviting incentive.**

Pickup artists are indirect in approach. They know they want to know the girl's demographics but they go at it indirectly by first drawing her engagement into something more unconsciously or innocently compelling.

I realise the good business relationships I have were with people I met indirectly; either through introduction by an acquaintance, over beer or useless banter. Hence golf is a popular way of networking.

When you catch up with people you met indirectly, the conversation can meander from serious (conscious) to casual and even silly (unconscious), in no particular order – because it has a casual foundation.

You all have seen the boring speaker (like I am) who goes on and on with the serious stuff, without detours or jokes so to bring his audience back to life.

2. Be comfortable with you

Rapport

Many times we fool ourselves that people in our space are comfortable talking to us because we desperately want them to. Read their body cues, the answer is there.

Our job in networking is to make them feel comfortable. Pickup artists call this 'building rapport'.

The pathway to good networking is to find commonalities or joiners (things that complement the other's interests). If you are talking to Bill Gates, maybe charity could be the commonality. A joiner could be a book you read on exponentially accelerating charity work.

Vulnerability

Pickup artists separate **vulnerability** in two ways: the one demonstrates high value and the other - low value. The former is when you tell that story of when you cried like a little baby after your soccer injury. The latter is when you relate the story of when you cried like a little baby, got down on the floor and begged your girlfriend not to leave you. I like the latter for my self-serving comedic interests – but you shouldn't.

Go on tell that story of when your first business venture went under: you were running away from the bank as they wanted to repossess your car and how you dodged the labour union. Paint the pain and determination you showed. I remember the days I had to revisit old roll-on bottles because I didn't have money, but still I went out did my thing.

3. See you as a person of value

Pickup artists would demonstrate value by showing girls their pictures with celebrities or pretty girls.

We know business people who pull similar tricks like sharing stories and pictures of when they travelled abroad. No matter what you think of it, it works in most cases.

Anyhow, if you have travelled the world and have interesting stories to share – that is your shtick.

Different paths of demonstrating value

Greeting people with an attentive attitude is conveying value.

Engaging people with curiosity (not condensation) in what they do is demonstrating value. Human's favourite topic is themselves.

"Everyone has an invisible sign hanging on their neck saying 'make me feel important'" Mary Kay Ash.

Connecting people who can help one another is demonstrating value. Directing people to good resources, e.g. manufacturers, is also it. First you would have found out what they do.

It is worthwhile to also check my previous posts on networking: How I Overcame Being a Bad Networker *http://buff.ly/1WA9zUe*

4. Like you

When you are able to open up and draw engagement in people, you are in baba, they like you.

5. Trust you

Once people like you and you have demonstrated value to them, it is easy to trust you.

People out there lie or pretend (pictures with celebrities) to get people's trust. They create stellar perceptions of themselves. It works.

I know a lot of people who get drawn into trading currencies because the forex dudes flaunt pictures living the life: Ferraris, Rolex watches, the sharp suits, 10 star hotels and and and.

That is social proof ladies and gentlemen.

I do not have authority over how anyone should win anyone's trust.

Tiisetso Maloma

Besides being flashy – if it is your thing, social proof can come in many other ways. Keep working and doing a good job. Keep adding value to people, with and without payment. The world will give testimony of your value. Testimonials are better branding than business cards and websites – they are social proof. Use testimonials.

I just want Hank Moody's Porsche.

- -

Richard Pryor was raped a couple of times as a kid, by a catholic priest at some point. He made it public knowledge and had a way of making fun of his tragic past. That right there is vulnerability and self deprecation.

People tend to be drawn to people who aren't afraid to be vulnerable, because shit happens in everyone's life though some don't share. They see those who talk as brave. Richard was brave. Bill Cosby didn't like crude humour; there are stories of him chastising crude comedians.

Not everyone likes those who come off talking about their vulnerabilities; they prefer those who pose shiny success. They good thing is, these people could be leeches. It is better when they are not attracted to you.

Pickup artists do not pick girls for lasting relationship (maybe). In business you want longevity and therefore one's honesty has to be consistent.

6. Do business with you

All this steps lead here.

- -

The opening sentence was just a ploy to **engage your attention** and to give myself my daily dose self-deprecation.

AVOID THESE EXPRESSIONS AND GESTURES TO WIN PEOPLE OVER IN PERSON, AS LEARNED FROM PICKUP ARTISTS

Here is what I did. I wrote a post titled How to Win People Over in Business through Pickup Artist Patterns. Check it out. I later figured since pickup artists are clinical readers of social dynamics (women or men for that matter), they would know what social cure gestures to avoid in order to be effective when engaging any audience in person.

The same points could possibly apply to networking or presentations.

I got on the net, looked for 'points to avoid' and to my luck I found '25 points' curated by Tyler Durden (Owen Cook). I selected those which would serve the purpose for this post.

The text in ITALICS is quoted.

You do not have to agree with all the points, I agree with most of them, some in certain cases. See this as information brought up for your selective benefit and choose what you think can improve you.

Fidgety movements and tight shoulders
It is a visible sign of being scared or stunned a bit. Loosen up the shoulders and relax yourself.

Talking too fast
You want to sneak in all that you want to say quickly because you are anxious they won't give you any further time.

Take it easy, to be in control of people - be in control of you.

Tiisetso Maloma

Laughing at your own jokes

It is tough when no laughs at your jokes, I know.

Saying "right" or "you know" after statements

This is seeking validation that what you said was heard and true.

Talking too softly or loud

Talking too soft: the fear that you are imposing yourself on people. You belong, believe and act like it.

Talking too loud: This is over compensating that you think you do not belong and therefore you have to prove you do.

Some people are loud naturally, it is fine.

The point here is to not over-do or under-do as a way of compensating for what you think you lack.

Leaning in or pecking

It is business networking, or are you trying to land a kiss? It is uncomfortable when people talk down your neck. Keep space.

Answering questions too early

It shows listening isn't really your interest. And who wants to talk to someone who rushes them and doesn't pay an ear?

Replying with overly thought-out of logical answers or with overly clear/formal pronunciation

It hints concern that you think you won't be accepted as you are, you aren't confident with your stuff and you don't gel with it. You then opt to sound scripted and like a robot.

Ooze your work, your majesty!

Taking too many sentences to state an idea that could be stated in less space

Qualifying yourself. Commander Zap emails me a few months ago: "Remember TD (Tyler Durden), don't write what you can say, don't say what you can wink, don't wink what you can smile" TIGHT. The shorter you can explain something; the more PROFOUND you'll appear. Why? You're not qualifying yourself.

The more we prepare and practice, the more concise and effective we become in explaining things. Let's practice.

Overcompensating insecurities

Fear of not being accepted. Have you ever met a janitor who the first thing he says is "money is over-rated. I would never get caught up in the corporate world" blah blah. If they'd have just said "I'm a janitor" and LEFT IT AT THAT we wouldn't have even THOUGHT that anything was wrong with it.. but because they INSTANTLY start overcompensating, it comes off as if they are qualifying themselves.

Same with if they BRING IT UP TOO EARLY. Like "hey, I'm Steve.. I'm a janitor and I love it".. They're TRYING to be cocky but it comes off as COMPENSATING.

Just be comfortable with yourself, and don't bring up overcompensating issues at all.

Overcompensating failure or shortcomings

Fear of being judged. If you have shitty clothes on, don't say "I have nicer clothes at home." Just don't bring it up.

LOL. You heard the above, don't bring it up man, don't. When you are in your little brother's VW Golf 1, don't say "I have a Merc at home".

WOMEN'S CREATIVITY SAVED THE WORLD, JILL SCOTT'S MOTHER AND HER POTATOES

The theme of my upcoming book, The Anxious Entrepreneur, is anxiety defeats creativity and creativity defeats anxiety.

Anxiety and creativity cannot exist in the same space; one must make room for the other.

The other day I was preparing food. I wanted something different to what I usually make or can make. Given the kind of food available, it was a bit tough to think an unusual dish. Plus, my creativity is limited in the kitchen.

August is women's month in South Africa and this connected to a story I heard Jill Scott share about her mother and upbringing on an interview with Mapaseka Mokwele on Kaya FM.

They didn't have much growing up. For some reason there were always potatoes in their house. Her mother would always amaze her with her creativity. Today she would make fries, the others wedges, soufflé, potato mash, etc.

Such creativity!

It is tough and troubling for a parent when there is no food in the house. They work with whatever is available, usually staple food, in a South African context it could be maize meal. They think all out to make different dishes with the same food type on different days.

They get their mind away from the stress of no food and step into a realm of creativity.

This morning it is normal maize-meal soft porridge; the following is maize-meal sour soft porridge (bogobe bja ting). Add some vinegar it is a different porridge for the other day.

Creativity saves any day. It trumps and chucks anxiety away.

Let's thank our mothers, or any women, for always being creative and whipping interesting dishes even if is of the same food type.

TWO WAYS ANXIETY CAN AFFECT ENTREPRENEURS

Becoming spam and a nuisance

When nothing is coming off your hustle, it can get you ticked off and anxious.

I have experienced this several times. I would start pitching people out of desperation to win, without thoughtfully weighing if what I am offering levels up to at least fair value for whoever I am pitching.

I become a nuisance.

When we do this, we become nothing but spam.

Can't add value

It is obvious, when the mind is focused on problems, it will stress further and deeper.

It can't think of creative solutions. Therefore it cannot add value.

To add value, it has to unwind.

It is that whole say that you can't think out of the box while you are in the box. You got to get out of the box.

That is why walks are said to be ideal for when you are stressed out.

BUT HE IS NIGERIAN: THE IMPORTANCE OF RELATING AN HONEST SCOPE WITH CLIENTS

I can build Wordpress websites. It is subject to debate though. I mess around with few easy themes and manipulate them until they look awesome. I cannot really edit CSS (the design code used on Wordpress websites).

The only reason I learned Wordpress a bit was because I needed a website and I could not afford a web designer. This is back in 2010 or so. I have been doing this since then till 2014.

It was the era of the branding epidemic. All the branding gurus said you need a website to be taken seriously. No you don't. Stay with this book I will show you.

There is so much bullshit out there of the things you 'must do' as an entrepreneur. Good bullshit and bad bullshit. Pick only the BS you want to use and run with it.

Anyway, they story is with this web designer reputation I got going around, a friend of mine, JohnJohn (not his real name), whom before I had build a website for referred me to a Nigerian guy called Jacob (not his real name) who runs a club in Johannesburg Sandton (I am not sure if it is popular or not).

Jacob wanted a website for his online entertainment magazine. We did the whole meeting, briefing and 50% deposit thing. And I am cheap - affordable baby.

This guy is huge hey, muscles and all, 6 to 8 feet. He is Nigerian.

This was good side money, I could not resist. It's back in 2012, the year I was broker than broke. He chose a theme. I start designing. He is one of those clients that contact you constantly to check progress, annoyingly so.

By the way, do not chat with clients via Whatsapp. The thing with it is people can see you are online and you haven't replied to their messages. It causes unnecessary tension. At least with emails, you can reply at a time you are ready to revert appropriately. Or even acknowledge receiving a mail and say you will reply in good time. And email leaves a manageable trail.

Of course I gave him timelines and I was sticking to them. All day he kept asking for progress updates via Whatsapp. This one morning I wake up to find these long Whatsapp messages of how lazy I am. He wants his money back and that if I don't refund him he will find me. Ooooohhh scary!

He is huge, runs a club and he is Nigerian. That is enough to scare me.

So I call my friends and relate the threats, they all go "he is just bluffing, don't give nothing back, you did work and that amounts to something".

I go like, "guys, but he is Nigerian". Oh gosh I am stereotyping.

I checked the website and he had taken it down. I worked on it the previous night till the morning. I did a bit to the website; I added plugins and changed colour schemes.

Remember I am not a website designer in the technical true sense; I am like a Wordpress themes editor.

He didn't like that I didn't do what website designers do, which is design to a point of almost changing a given theme.

How did it end, let us say I didn't pay back all his deposit and my friend who referred me had to get involved.

The lessons

It is ok to make side money or do whatever business. Your experience does not matter more than honesty of what you can deliver.

Since then I have designed Wordpress websites for many people, the difference since then is I am upfront from the start as to what my capabilities are and what I can deliver. I play around with themes until they look good, I cannot do deep coding.

These folks I did websites for, I have realised, didn't want the best website in the world; they just wanted a minimally viable site.

You will find that when you are honest with what you can do, people will use you still.

This is side money for me, hopefully not anymore. I do not market such services but clients keep coming.

I do not want to design websites. But I do, it is fun.

MAKING A DIRTY JOKE AND THE ONLY 4 THINGS I LEARNED FROM GILBERT GOTTFRIED

He is labelled a 'comedian's comedian'. I am new to Gilbert Gottfried's comedy. I first learned of it on *Comedy Central* Roast of David Hasselhof, and later on that of Hugh Hefner. Since then I have been zooming into his acts.

I realised I have seen him before in the movie *The Problem Child* where he played an adoption agent and in *Aladdin* as the parrot Iago.

"I have always said my career is somewhere between children's programming and hard-core porn" Gilbert.

Some say he makes dirty and disgusting jokes. Well he has an album called *Dirty Jokes*.

I am a total fan of his often number 1 (iTunes) Amazing Colossal Podcast where he interviews personalities with insights into old Hollywood. It can delve into 1960's actors and comedians.

Here are lessons I take from Gilbert Gottfried.

He does not back down
Being a stand-up comedian must be one of the hardest acts in life. Making people laugh for 30 minutes plus - let alone 10 minutes - cannot be easy.

I have heard a few comedians salute Gilbert for not backing down from a hard crowd with easy jokes.

An example of going for easy jokes is in the movie *Funny People* where Ira (Seth Rogan) – an upcoming comedian, goes on stage after George Simmons's (Adam Sandler) strange and dark act –a successful comedian who just discovered he has a death disease and so goes performing at small clubs to sort of say goodbye to the world. He finds it hard to crack the audience with the material he prepared; he then opts for the easy jabs by making fun of George's surprisingly peculiar act.

Self deprecation

Knowing how to take laughs from deprecating yourself is a special trait. We take ourselves seriously. Having the ability to not only laugh at ourselves but self deprecate is relieving.

"I can't even find someone for a platonic relationship, much less the kind where someone wants to see me naked" Gili.

I always hear Gilbert take jabs at himself on the podcast: his looks, comic abilities (lack of), career (its death) and acting (terrible).

I once heard him make a joke of how Hollywood producers are liars. Some once expressed liking towards him for a movie role, which they later gave to Dustin Hoffman. The joke is, the only time his name is ever mentioned in the same sentence with Dustin Hoffman's is when people say *"I have seen Gilbert's acting and he is no Dustin Hoffman"*.

Gilbert has no acting skills or language skill or any skills. What a bunch of unceremoniously vindictive and lying Hollywood producers.

We are merely taking chances in this world, the world reacts how it wants and taking ourselves seriously all the time invites agonising disappointment.

He does what he loves fully and to the end

"Find what you love and let it kill you". Apparently *Charles Bukowski said this*.

Well, what Gilbert loves – comedy, has got him fired. He is still doing it. *"Although now I do think twice before I say something, even though I go ahead and say it anyway"* Gilbert.

He has been performing standup since he was 15 years of age. Wikipedia says he is now 61. He is still performing at nightclubs.

Don Rickles is 89 and is still performing.

Gilbert often say, his comic references were old when he started (1955 maybe?) and even today they are still of that era.

Doesn't ask for permission (pays it forward)

Standup comedy does not require much permission. You write jokes and find anywhere to perform them for free. You can bomb a couple of times, but as long as you keep practicing, you will get your swing.

Gilbert started performing at 15 doing mostly voice impersonations, obviously without pay. He has been working on it ever since, and today is he is 61.

If the clubs say no to you, there is YouTube and Facebook video. Or whatever channels that allow you to broadcast your craft.

It applies to when you are a musician or writer.

Some people go to school, study PR and wait for an employment opportunity. You do not have to wait. You can increase your employment opportunities by paying it forward, doing stuff for free. Go out solicit 'pay it forward' opportunities.

Paying it forward allows you to be noticed, attractive and more wanted. It gets you to a point where you give others permission to use your skills, unlike you asking for the allowance.

- -

Maybe 4 points are not much, but I personally espouse to have these traits until old age. Doing stuff around what you love is fulfilling.

I might have learned to make dirtier, more insulting and more taboo jokes from Gilbert.

Here is my portrait of a Gilbert Gottfried inspired joke

Would you like to hear a dirty joke about a jealous toothless man?

A man is walking down the street, he trips and falls.

A toothless man and a handless man are watching him.

Before he hits the ground, he manages to stretch out his hands and balances out the fall.

Only his knees are hurt and his trouser is dirty dirty.

The toothless man laughs hard and says, "you lucky sonaofab*..., I wished you would have fell on your teeth and knocked them all out".

The handless man starts laughing uncontrollably at the toothless man and says "let me guess, you used your teeth to balance out falls?"

What a jealous toothless man.

WHY YOU DO QUALIFY TO DO WHATEVER YOU WANT

People are afraid to pursue their ambitions. They think they lack the authority and expertise.

I have seen a lot of them hide behind acquiring further knowledge – be it schooling, attending more conferences, networking. Nothing is wrong with these activities – it is actually bright to do them. Just they should not be an excuse for not starting.

Your background does not determine whether you can do it or not

Steve Jobs was not a programmer and apparently he never did code. But he founded and ran technology companies. He had idea uses. He got partners who could produce. Then he pursued ferociously.

Elon Musk studied physics and economics in tertiary. He wasn't the best programmer probably. Apparently when his company Zip2 expanded, *"new software engineers had to rewrite the codebase due to the poor coding methodology used by Musk"*.

I doubt if my homeboy Musk cares much about he himself being the best programmer or car mechanic. His obsession is making idea uses come to life – a lot of them.

There are shortcuts to breaking into different industries. Getting a partner who can program or hiring is a shortcut if you want to start a tech company.

Even, the internet is filled with **shortcut** coding lessons or whatever lessons for that matter: speaking, writing, marketing, carpentry etc.

Again I believe in learning for a purpose (action), i.e. if you want to do a specific product, learn how to build the specific product whilst building it.

- It is more interesting and you learn specifics – which saves time.
- You become a product use expert, i.e. as you test the product in the market, you learn what works, what users want and conceive other uses.
- You are the one who takes the product to the market – good businessmen are trained in this fashion.
- Versus going to school for a 3 year degree, in this way, in a year you could learn how to build 3 products. You will have the opportunity to fail or succeed in sales, marketing, relationship maintaining, networking, cash flow, etc. You would have learned what to do and not do – breakthroughs and discoveries happen in between these. School only teaches you what to do.

Products are about use, not expertise nor authority. Expertise can be hired, rented or partnered in. Authority is bi-product of action.

Do it if you care about it

I am not a rich entrepreneur, but what the fuck qualifies me to write a book on entrepreneurship titled 'Forget The Business Plan Use This Short Model'. Or a book called 'The Anxious Entrepreneur'.

The deal is I cared so much about entrepreneurship. So I became one. Through hard knocks, I learned what to do and not do. At the end of those days, I still gave a damn about entrepreneurship. I am still one even today.

Then I realised a business plan is a useless teaching tool. Everyone (the entrepreneurs) thought so. The discussions in between, of what works and matters (validation) – then became the book 'Forget The Business Plan Use This Short Model'.

I now sell the book to aspiring entrepreneurs and entrepreneurs.

If something is true for you, true for a niche, you care about it; then it is enough to invest in creating a product out of it. This is what the Elons and Steve's of this world did.

They did it a number of times. I am sure they failed at certain adventures.

Mark Cuban puts it this way: "It doesn't matter how many times you fail. It doesn't matter how many times you almost get it right. No one is going to know or care about your failures, and neither should you. All you have to do is learn from them and those around you because... All that matters in business is that you get it right once. Then everyone can tell you how lucky you are."

No product is perfect

If you ask any car manufacturer if they made the best cars, they will outright say "YES". Yet we have seen millions of cars being recalled for one fault or another. Toyota, Kia, Isuzu, Chevy and who else? Now VW has been caught for installing some emission cheating software.

I am certain McDonalds has recalled thousands of burgers over the years – if not millions.

If you were at McDonalds right now and you caught a fly dead in your meal (hopefully not a cockroach), you then brought it to their attention - they will say "sorry" without maybe really accepting the blame. But they will make it up to you by offering a replacement meal or refund if that is what you seek.

No product is 100% solid perfect. The gage is it needs to be good enough for use and with a slight differentiator at least (either price, quality, location and whatever works in that given case) – the weak links can be serviced and maintained.

The car makers, the cell phone makers, they do not produce all components they use themselves. They outsource what is available and what is available is not necessarily the best. The best is yet to be made. So every year, while operating, they search for the next best component to be made.

Even Tesla is searching for that perfect battery. But they are on the ground running (not waiting) as a motor company already.

Since no product is stunning perfect, why are you waiting until yours is Godly? Get on the ground and run – better ideas will come. Don't be afraid to do it -- and make up for it like McDonalds and the car manufacturers.

"Action precedes creativity" Grand Cardone.

Fear

It would be ingenuine not to address fear. There was never a point where I was about to put out a book or whatever product and I didn't feel scared. Fear that people won't like it and will tell it to my face. Fear that it isn't good enough to be on shelves. What if they say my product won't work – it is poorly designed - I lack expertise? My stomach turns when these thoughts visit.

I was reading that Stephen Dubner, author of Freakonomics, was shit scared before it came out. Well it went to sell over 5 million copies.

Fear is real. Let's not fight it. But, for instance if it's a book, I know if work hard on it – I vet each concept critically – I am **honest** - and I write blog posts (not book posts) almost every day (to practice), I will have an honest product.

There is no way of testing yourself and growing as entrepreneur if you don't put your product out there. No product no entrepreneur. So fear just has to take a back sit, however powerful it is.

Although failure is undesirable, it is a better builder of men than success.

It is not so much that trying tests potential, it is that trying builds and exercises potential. As sportsmen get fit through training, so do entrepreneurs when they try.

We will never exercise our potential if we don't try, if we don't put anything out.

So you there you have it, failure, whatever imposes it - won't you get you anywhere but nowhere.

Take it from me, being laughed isn't nice. But being able to laugh at myself is another thing. It is a fantastic high and it kind of makes up for everything. It discharges a renewed and robust spirit to try again.

Success is...

Those we call successful (the millionaire definition) made products (not the most perfect), sold a lot to make millions and offered after sales care. That's all. Think about it!

I felt a bit hurt when I heard one author (I cannot recall who) say: to have a best-seller, write another book and another until you become one. As you keep writing and marketing, your breakout book will spiral on the previous books. I am on my third book; it is called The Anxious Entrepreneur. Pre-order it here. My next book will be called Pride Economics; it comes out 2016 or 2017. I will be doing this for a long while.

"Do what you love and let it kill you"

Are you going to let the fear of lack authority-ship stop you from doing what you want to do? Do you want to be killed by what you do not want to do? There should always be a tit bit of what you love in your everyday, until it takes over. I am saying even if you start small but as long as what you love factors into your day.

THE MAN WHO FED HIS CHILD WITH THE FACE OF THE MOTHER, A METAPHOR FOR CREATIVITY

No, it wasn't The Joker.

Below is the man. He needs a name, let's call him Sy.

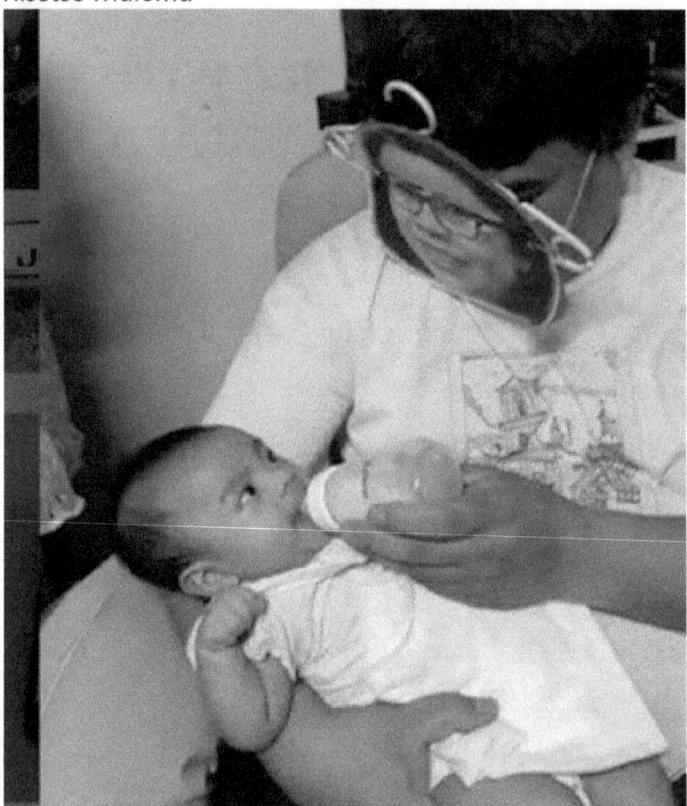

The big question is why did this gentleman feed the child with the baby mama's face?

No, he did not feed the mom's actual face to the child. You can see he stuck a picture of the mother to his face as to deceive the toddler into believing it was the mama doing the feeding.

I guess children are deceivable. At times I wonder if I am not a child as Instagram filters sometimes do dupe me.

The background thoughts
When I first saw this image going around on social media I had a couple of thoughts:

-      Maybe he is the new nanny

- He is the father, the mother dumped the kid with him

The thoughts can go on and on.

It does not matter what the situation or relation is. If you are babysitting and it is time to feed the child, and it does not want to eat – it will stress you.

We know stress doesn't conceive solutions. Then it is time to get creative and peddle possible solutions to make the child eat.

Our friend Sy got creative. The other ideas he might have thought are:

- Dance whilst feeding the baby. Babies tend to love movement, especially when it is out of sync.
- Sing or play for the baby its supposed favourite song.
- Put the mother on the phone loudspeaker so she can talk while he feeds the little one.

He went with putting a picture of the mother (or mother figure) on his face so to deceive the little crying star.

Think of this picture as metaphor for 'creativity defeats anxiety'. The anguish of not knowing what to do to solve a problem is anxiety. Sy defeated the anxiety by getting creative.

THE UNTOLD GENIUS OF THE TRAFFIC-LIGHT JOB SEEKER CHEMIST

This post was originally a Facebook post on my page.

I heard this young lady, Malwandla Hadebe, got a call from Sasol after her pictures of attracting a job street-beggar-like went viral. I hope they offer her employment.

Let's try digesting the following perspective, just to see if it fits.

Obviously unemployment in the country is a serious and immediate challenge. A picture like this colours the severity and unfairness of the situation, i.e. engineering graduates having to beg for jobs - beggar-like.

As society we feel emotional, sympathetic and helpless.

Maybe let's look at the picture without the helplessness... This lady is a genius. She marketed herself good

85

- She marketed herself and went viral by mixing two worlds or demographics that make an oxymoron (for lack of a better description): i.e. begging (associated with helplessness) and university-engineering-graduate (associated with highly-sought-after-value)

- Add to the pot a demographic of 'societal sympathy' and virality is ignited

- Any company that offers her employment in the midst of this virality gets 'societal favour' or call it PR. Thus all parties win as everybody looks good: employer, society and the lady.

Give the lady RESPEK for her genius. The normal ways of landing a job (sending CV's, going to companies, etc) weren't working. So she upped the ante and threw in a more 'dramatic' manoeuvre. She's a high thinker and risk taker.

All the best to her and all unemployed graduates.

Dear graduate, learn how to market yourself. Attract opportunities to yourself.

TO SOUTH AFRICAN BRANDPRENEURS: 'SUPPORT LOCAL' IS A WEAK AMMUNITION

Let's be honest, do you support local than what you love (which is mostly international stuff)? If you do, you are an uncelebrated hero.

Even the unions' (Cosatu, Num, Numsa etc.) investment arms do not invest in local young start-ups. I do not know these for a fact – I am an ars...

I used to own and run 2 labels: gabble heights and Rural Joss. Most people who bought our clothes did so because they loved the brand: design, fabric, intrigue, appeal and fit. This is all from feedback. I am sure there were those who bought because we were local guys and others because they were our friends.

But I am definitely sure those who bought out of fascination with far out weighted those who supported out of 'buy local'.

Lets us take All Star Converse as an example. It is an American brand. It is loved everywhere else in the world, especially here in South Africa. In the past it used to be associated with ma-pantsula, but now it appeals to a lot different sub-cultures. Actually it cuts across sub-cultures. For some people, they just have to have it.

When a South African buys All Star, it is because it intrigues them in one way or another. Whether it's that it looks good on them or that it is in trend or it is their signature.

When an American buys it, either one or all of these reasons apply. The nationality of the brand could to an extend bear weight (I think it's extremely little), but I am sure it is not a determining factor – it is just a bonus: the shoe's intrigue, look and appeal outweigh the brand's geographical roots.

Hence Americans can love many other European brands: Versace Versace Versace Versace Versace –or whatever number of times that songs says Versace. It is a product's intrigue which determines if a sale is made.

Loxion Kulca

I remember H2O's 2003 (am I right?) 'wonderful' video. It featured a whole lot of South African celebrities wearing Loxion Kulca. We immediately loved the brand either because of its appeal, design, meaning (especially for a resurging SA), intrigue and the famous stylish people who wore it. Zandi Nhlapo boss. The 'proudly local' factor came last, if it came – it was just a bonus.

I am not dictating how people should run their brands, but what I think will stand out is: design, meaning, appeal, intrigue and whatever reaction it gets out of people. But I strongly believe you cannot bank on the 'buy local' tag.

It is time we start making products which are just good on the basis of they are good.

We need as a country, to create a foundation for young entrepreneurs to start businesses of compelling value. Entrepreneurial education is schools is mere enterprising i.e. buying and selling what is available or making what the entrepreneur feels is needed – not what is usable and needed by society. When I say compelling value I mean, businesses which are not compelling because they are proudly made in SA by a South African, but because they honestly intrigue interest in people/consumers to own them and/or use their value – here and beyond South Africa.

People buy the kind of compelling value which beats substitute (competition) products with one factor or more. We can agree Blackberry is a crappy phone, but some people still buy it over (or with) Samsung and Apple because of BIS, and maybe that it has cheaper versions. I know I do. Therefore Blackberry has a feasible 'compelling value' given its better competition.

But please, buy my book *'Forget The Business Plan Use This Short Model'* because it is 'proudly local'.

TWO WAYS FOR AFRICA TO GROW EXPONENTIALLY – PART 1

One way to define Africa's challenge is a lot of **us** do not know how to embed ourselves in the world economy, provide innovatively and freely without trying to rope in perceived gatekeepers.

Online Shipping System that Quotes Buyers Instantly to Anywhere in the World

At the backdrop of the South African Post Office having 'going concern' challenges, there are a number of local courier companies mushrooming. Interesting!

I am still not over the pain SAPO cost my book business last year when they went on strike for months.

We do not have bookstore distribution for my books in South Africa or across Africa. We use SAPO to ship. The post office is relatively cheaper. I so wish they had an instant online shipment-quoting-system, instead of having to go to them every time. Even better, a shopper instructed quoting system you can plug into web stores.

It got me thinking that the ability to sell online via an online store, where the customers, anywhere in the world, can instantly get a shipping quote, can be exponential for Africa's growth.

We did some little research of what is available out there as I have a book coming up - The Anxious Entrepreneur. Plus we would like to promote and sell it to African countries buzzing with startup entrepreneurs: SADEC countries, Kenya, Rwanda, Nigeria, Ghana and others.

There is Shopify. Anyone can setup an online store instantly with it. Then we discovered a courier company called Dawn Wing, they have a free Shopify plugin. Anyone can set up a store there with capabilities to give instant shipping quotes to anywhere in the world.

Tiisetso Maloma

Imagine this power that any creator of products in Africa can setup an online store instantly and have automatic international shipping. This is what free markets are about.

It won't matter whom their marketing reaches. They can get it to them.

Think of this point as a metaphor for 'freedom to access'. These days we do not have to buy billboards (expensive and unaffordable to startups) to access markets. There is Facebook Ads, wherein for R10 a day, you can advertise to your selected niche and reach over a 500 people.

Teaching Coding to Primary School Kids

My generation of high scholars (I am 28), I suspect even the current generation, cannot readily identify how their subjects work into their lives now and in future careers.

Back in high school I could not figure how to apply geometry, accounting or science to my life situation - then and in future.

Many years later as an entrepreneur, I find myself learning things with a purpose. I read marketing articles so I can know effective ways of promoting products. The only way maths applied to my life then was it is for learning at school and practicing at home – nothing outside.

There is something about coding (computer programming). I do not, cannot and do not want to code. But I can readily understand the purpose it serves in most things I use daily: mobile phone, DSTV decoder (I possess one but do not have a television), Buffer App (for scheduling tweets), printer, ebook reader, etc.

It basically runs most things in life today and more so in the future. The beer we drink is made with programmed machines. The cars we drive. Robots. Microwaves.

If kids in primary and high schools can be taught basic programming and its possible uses, as they go through their days, they will realise most things are programmed: electric toys, music players, games, etc.

The thing which will stand out is the different purposes for which programming is used for and can be used for.

Their basic of programming will always connect with workings of different products and their purposes. They will see deficiencies in workings of programmed products and get a sense they can improve them. Then they will get ideas of what uses they program for.

I read story of 2 kid brothers in Nigeria (Osine - 13 and Anesi Ikhianosime - 15) who taught themselves coding and created a web browser enhanced for feature and low end phones because they were "fed up with Google Chrome". They saw a deficiency that international web browsers aren't enhanced for Africa's slow internet. The web browser is called Crocodile Browser Lite and is available on the Google Play store.

I believe the leading drive for learning coding wasn't necessarily to just have the skill but the perceived purposes (ideas) for which they can use it for. The internet is abundant with free coding lessons and shortcuts.

When people understand the purpose for which a skill can serve, they are be motivated to self teach.

If African kids can be introduced coding in primary and high school, the world then has millions of coders who will contribute to newer uses of coding, improve deficiencies in workings of products and do so at own driven will – which is entrepreneurial.

I think of Wordpress (open source website creation and hosting tool/application) and the thousands of plugins (add-on software component that adds specific features to an existing software application) it has, created by private individuals. They offer them partially free but you have to purchase to get their full use.

Even Shopify has private coders for profit.

There are plugins for website sign-up forms, product order forms, videos displaying, shopping carts, etc. Imagine if African kids were up in there competing and contributing. The rest of Africa (and the world) would be up in there benefiting. Jobs would be self created.

Kids of 10 years could independently be able to contribute economically by 17 years and prior tertiary.

This is how the next Mark Shuttleworths will come out. He knew coding and coded for a purpose. Look where it got him.

OBSERVING 15 POINTS OF THE ASCENDANCE OF JULIUS MALEMA

Some saw the rise of young Nelson Mandela and the victory of old Nelson become the president of the first democratically elected government of South Africa in 1994 - at the age of 75.

Not all who saw the young Nelson rise witnessed his presidency of course; 75 is a lot of years to be around living.

It so happens our generation is witnessing the rise of another politician, Julius Malema.

The young Julius Malema from Limpopo, carrying a gun at age 13 to go burry the late struggle hero and communist leader Chris Hani in 1993; to leading a Jozi shut down march as president of Cosas in 2002; to heading the ANC Youth League as president – breaking recruitment milestones, expulsion from the ANC and setting up a party that within twelve months of start-up becomes the 3rd largest in parliament – out of many parties that have been in existence for years.

As an entrepreneur, I would like to think Alon Musk is great, but I can't play down play Julius' ascendance in his field of industry.

Not to say Julius is a Nelson Mandela, but in our age and South African politics, whether you are fond of him or not, he is a stat that stands out.

If I were a politician in any party - Julius Malema is the guy to envy even if I didn't agree with his ideas or wish to be him. Well maybe not for you because your envy temperament is even, so tranquil it puts the Dalai Lama's to shame. If you aren't envious, just know I can bite both my wrists at the same time, hahaha.

I am not with any political party, being South African and loyal to it only is enough to me. Politicians are often loyal first to their political parties and often later to their countries.

When a politician does wrong – corruption, often their party's first call is to protect organisation's image, not necessarily the country. Such imagery is needed to win votes from the citizens. It is bizarre how our psychology as society works.

Whatever you think of Julius Malema - he is doing his thing at a high level. The following isn't glorification, but simply observations of his ascendance.

Change of mind!!

"A wise man changes his mind", said the wise man adjusting his earlier views.

Malema was a Jacob Zuma backer. Today he is detractor. The temperament hasn't changed, if not gone up.

Captivating oratory.

When Julius speaks, he doesn't let you sleep. He gets serious, technical, silly, insulting and then back again to serious.

Good speakers do this (maybe without the insults). They own your attention's flow to their advantage.

The greatest of masters of ceremonies and attention, comedians, concede to that he is a good comedian.

Well play of the PR game.

Malema's orations, most times if not all the time, end up high up in the headlines.

The overt silliness and insults make good headline copy. He is his own copywriter.

Below are just few of the things Julius has said, which have made headlines and or were used as punch lines in media reports:

- Malema vows that once they appeal the court interdict they will surprise the Guptas with a visit.
- EFF will help Zuma deliver his speech!
- "SARS will soon auction my twitter because they want to take away everything I have"
- "King Dalindyebo is a friend of the EFF, but we respect the law and need for justice"
- "Jacob Zuma built a 2 million rand swimming pool, but no one in the family knows how to swim"
- "That which you have covered in [your] clothes is rubbish, ok! You are a small boy you can't do anything. Go out...bastard! Go out! You bloody agent!"
- "We are used like toilet paper that is flushed in the toilet. We are used like condoms -- those who use condoms will know how condoms work, they use them and they throw them [away] somewhere else"
- "She is a cockroach... She dances like a monkey"
- "Comrades, people have said it's cold outside the ANC, they are correct, they were correct, it's very cold outside the ANC...but we are making it warm"
- "You must never buy an E-Tag, when they stop you and ask you about your E-Tag, simply show them your red beret"

Ability to apologise and criticise self.

In 2014, he apologised to former President Thabo Mbeki's mother for how they "ill treated her child (Thabo)" leading to the president stepping down in 2008.

Earlier this year in parliament, he apologised to Mbeki for backing Zuma.

In 2011, while in Thebelihle, in strengthening his point, he referred to Indians in the C word. It is a derogatory slur and of course there was outrage. He says he did not know it is; growing up I also did not know until a few years prior Malema's incident.

South African Minority Rights Equality Movement (Samrem) opened a case of crimen injuria against him.

He then requested a meeting with them where he apologised. Samrem welcomed it.

Obscenity obviously attracts attention. So is apologising, even if lesser.

Nonetheless, if you think you were wrong, it is decent to apologise.

You don't have to play an opponent's preferred game to win a challenge

Lindiwe Mazibuko at some point challenged Julius to a debate. Julius's reply was, "She's a nobody, she's a tea girl of the madam".

"I was never asked to debate Lindiwe. I am not going to use our profile to profile her. She is a tea girl for the madam — she must stay there in the kitchen"

Whether he was afraid of her or not, some might argue, to me it makes no difference. The reply was hitting — even more so comically.

To win a challenge, you don't have to play the exact game the challenger suggests.

Again we can say: if you wrestle a pig, you are a pig; if you challenge a lion to a wrestle, even if you are not the king of the jungle, you are playing the big game — even when you are a porky.

Driven by ambitions, not lacks

We laughed when we heard he failed woodwork in Matric. He got a G in standard grade.

The jokes were funny.

People fail in school and let that define what happens with their life. They let tests that others put up for them determine whether they should go forward in life or not.

He pursued what he wanted in life - politics.

I am not certain if the woodwork jokes are still funny now that he obtained university degrees.

Consistency and perseverance

We can say that his tune hasn't changed from when he was the leader of ANCYL. Some even say he was expelled from the ANC for ferociously pushing the agenda of nationalisation of mines. This is the song he is still singing today and stronger.

Consistency is attractive to the world and perseverance builds the individual's stamina.

Find wounds of society

ABSA, a South African bank, whose controlling stake is owned by UK's Barclays Bank, apparently 'imported' 500 consultants, overlooking South African talent.

EFF threatened to stage sit-ins at ABSA branches, as part of their plan to force capitalism to transform urgently. The strategy is, to eat an elephant (banks), bite it in bits. ABSA happens to be the elephant they promised to start with.

A group of ABSA stuff in management apparently met with the ANC and later the EFF, seeking help in addressing the 'overlooking' matter.

Apparently 2800 employees signed a petition to join Malema's protest.

EFF wins this call over ANC. It is better suited to be radical. Cry beloved ANCYL.

After the above, as of March 2016, Barclays announced its process of disinvestment from ABSA. I am not saying this is due to the aforementioned.

When tables turn, enemies can be friends

Andile Mngxitama and Malema were sometimes at loggerheads.

After Malema got fired from the ANC, Andile was one the people he met up with in talks of new political party, which now is the EFF and which they are the founding members to. Well, Andile later left the EFF.

Ear on the ground

I am from Limpopo. I hang around 'comrades'. The banter veers into politics. We are a politically inclined nation.

I often hear people say Malema still has spies in the ANC. This is just gossip but doesn't mean it isn't true.

The interesting point I heard is Malema is a 'gents' guy. He would often call comrades just to check up on them.

Sense of urgency (48 Laws of Power)

He wants nationalisation now - today, not tomorrow. He wants land for people now, not tomorrow.

His EFF isn't the governing party so there is nothing they can do government policy wise.

We have seen land grabs in some communities apparently led by them. The government in some of those communities later came to officially give 'the people' the land.

People want their lives to improve today; hence they go with someone who wants change NOW.

The ANC isn't saying anything urgent about nationalisation of natural resources or at least an exponential beneficiation programme.

Lead a crusade (48 Laws of Power)

Remember the ANCYL march in 2011, from Johannesburg to the Union Buildings in Pretoria? I was a big twitterer then. I saw people, some prominent, who were openly not Malema fans at the march or sympathizing with it. Some said they were even shedding 'a tear'. I had FOMO, and I almost shed a tear.

Although we know the march wasn't going to create jobs or even immediately, we sympathized with the bigger meaning.

A crusade is defined as "a concerted effort or vigorous movement for a cause or against an abuse".

I went to the #FeesMustFall march, I am not a student. I sympathize greatly. I believe in the fees falling crusade – it is bigger than me.

Strategy over sense of occasion and comfort

Had the Nkandla issue been handled apologetically from the start, maybe the country wouldn't view the president with distain as it does now.

The attitude and tricks used to not apply the Public Protector's recommendations (they are binding by law) was the straw.

In the opening State of the Nation Address, the EFF hackled once more until they were booted out of the parliament.

There are those who viewed the EFF's behaviour as 'inappropriate' given the occasion.

The bigger 'inappropriate' is shielding the paying back of the millions abused on Nkandla.

The EFF never agreed to the Adhoc committee on Nkandla from the onset. That was their strategy.

Their view in my view is, unless the matter is addressed appropriately with respect of people's intellect and constitution, the 'strategy' would rule over and above any sense of occasion.

Detail

Malema's reply at the State of the Nation debate on 17/02/2016: the points which made headlines where attacks on President Zuma's personal life and the last words - "bye bye" and the sort of gimmickry stuff.

These were the last points of the speech. The first ¾ is a detailed analysis which speaks reality of South Africa current social and economic position.

The same can be said of EFF's recent trip to London, were Malema and colleagues met with the business community (investors) and students to promote or lobby their 'economic freedom' vision.

Charisma might win popularity, but detail engages decision makers - whom are practical.

Various business people, for self vested reasons or not, foresaw that an apartheid state's collapse was inevitable – possibly in a bad way if not contained - led the route to peace talks. No matter their race, they were not swayed by empty sentiments like 'whites would rule South Africa until until'.

Play field experience (from practice) and its mobilisation

It is not luck that the EFF got to party number 3 in parliament in less 12 months of being founded.

Even if the argument is they must have being long plotting, it also would speak to the fact that they know the political mobilising play field of South Africa and provinces.

Malema used to post ANC posters in the 1994 election (the first democratic elections in South Africa). His understanding of street logistics and mobilising must have started from there. He would have been around 13 years of age.

The Sasco 2002 Johannesburg shut down march speaks to this point.

EFF has more branches and in all the provinces than most of the parties in found in parliament. It achieved this in less than 2 years. The easy guess is they do not have funds as the ANC and the DA – how the hack did the achieve this?

The other guess is, since its some guys also from the ANC, they know how to hack growth numbers and they are young. Old politicians lose touch with the streets.

SEVEN RIDICULOUS THINGS I'VE NOTICED ABOUT THE GAUTRAIN

This is just observational satire. It isn't a piece about some measured criticism a transport export would give.

Gautrain is a top of the line transporter in Mzansi (South Africa), after planes. I am being patriotic here; hence I am not affording credit to Uber.

People stand on their feet

No one stands up in a mini bus taxi; but in the Gautrain you do.

It doesn't matter if you are the CEO of whatever top notch entity, you stand if there is not space. How unfortunate.

Gautrain seats are smaller than Toyota Quantum's

Yes they are. I have measured them, with my eyes.

Some of the announcements

I am sitting there at the station waiting for a train. Then I hear the announcements voice say, paraphrasing, "please do not hold the train doors from closing, it leads to delays in your journey".

If I am already inside the train, I wouldn't disrupt the doors from closing would I. It is only when I am outside trying to forge a way inside that I would hold the doors if the button isn't stopping them.

Therefore I would not be disrupting my journey – I would be trying to have one.

Stuffiness is allowed

I once commuted the train with marathon runners who were from some Spar race. Boy was it stinky stuffy.

Tiisetso Maloma

In the past I have witnessed taxi drivers return passengers' money and ask them to get off because the other commuters were complaining of the individual's 'stank'.

I give it up to the taxi drivers; they put through their requests (command) gracefully.

The station that is in Alexandra township is called Marlboro

When you leave the Marlboro station and step outside the gates, you realise you are in Alexandra – not Marlboro.

That is extension 10 in Alex. Marlboro is few metres away.

Yes ladies and gentlemen, the Gautrain folks thought it would be a bad branding exercise to say the prestigious train has a station in the township Alexandra.

People don't greet

I once heard a taxi driver say to some lady who got into our taxi and did not close the door behind her: "you don't close the door behind you, you don't greet, you are wearing a frown face – this isn't Gautrain".

Ubuntu dololo in the Gautrain.

Airport commuters are always running late

With every Gautrain trip, there are always 2 or more people running with shame to catch the train to OR Tambo International Airport.

Aren't these people supposed to be more responsible than the most of society? I mean they can afford to fly and surely hold a senior role at work.

- -

You roast the ones you love. Xap xap.

Bonus: 2 facts you might not have known about transport in South Africa

Putco bus

If you didn't know, each seat in a Putco bus has an owner. If you just got a new job, you can't just buy a ticket and go seat anywhere.

Kulula

You can open the windows and wing-hang your out out. How cool is that?

www.ingramcontent.com/pod-product-compliance
Lightning Source LLC
Chambersburg PA
CBHW070326190526
45169CB00005B/1762

9 781535 103138